Rivers

Written by Sally Hewitt

W

First published in 2009 by Franklin Watts
338 Euston Road, London NW1 3BH

Franklin Watts Australia
Level 17/207 Kent Street, Sydney NSW 2000

Copyright © Franklin Watts 2009

Editor: Katie Dicker
Art Direction: Dibakar Acharjee (Q2AMedia)
Designer: Shruti Aggarwal, Neha Kaul (Q2AMedia)
Picture researcher: Kamal Kumar (Q2AMedia)
Craft models made by: Tarang Saggar (Q2AMedia)
Photography: Dibakar Acharjee (Q2AMedia)

Picture credits:
t=top b=bottom c=centre l=left r=right

Cover: Shutterstock.
Title page: Wonganan Sukcharoenkana/Istockphoto.
Insides: Juan Carlos Munoz/Photolibrary: 6,
Maksym Gorpenyuk/Shutterstock: 7b, Yann Arthus-
Bertrand/Corbis: 9t, Laurin Rinder/Shutterstock: 10t,
Alfgar/Shutterstock: 10b, Diego Azubel/
IndiaPicture/EPA: 12t, Bojan Brecelj/Corbis: 12b,
Wonganan Sukcharoenkana/Istockphoto: 14,
Maxstockphoto/Shutterstock: 15br,
Graeme Knox/Shutterstock: 16t, Shutterstock: 16b,
Robert Ellis/Istockphoto: 18, Victoria McCormick/
Photolibrary: 19t, Tyler Olson/Shutterstock: 20t,
Sergey Mostovoy/123RF: 20b, Patrick Ward/Corbis:
22t, Patrick Armstrong/Big Stock Photo: 22b,
Joel W. Rogers/Corbis: 24t, Evron/Shutterstock: 24b,
Vito Lee/Reuters: 26, Paul Glendell/Alamy: 27t,
Geoffrey Kuchera/Shutterstock: 27b.
Q2AMedia Image Bank: Imprint page, Contents page,
9, 11, 13, 15, 17, 19, 21, 23.
Q2AMedia Art Bank: 7, 8, 17, 19, 25.

With thanks to our model Shruti Aggarwal.

A CIP catalogue record for this book
is available from the British Library.

ISBN: 978 0 7496 8768 7

Dewey Classification: 551.48'3

Printed in China

Franklin Watts is a division of Hachette Children's
Books, an Hachette UK company.
www.hachette.co.uk

Contents

What is a river? 6

All along a river 8

Wearing away the land 10

Flood plains 12

Bends and loops 14

River plants 16

River wildlife 18

Using rivers 20

River transport 22

Enjoying rivers 24

Caring for rivers 26

Glossary 28

Index 30

Words that appear in **bold** can be found in the glossary on pages 28–29.

What is a river?

A river is a wide stream of water flowing downhill over land to the sea. Rivers flow along **channels** that can be straight or winding, wide or narrow, deep or shallow.

Longest and biggest!

The world's longest river is the River Nile in Africa. It is 6,671 kilometres long. The Amazon River in South America is 6,440 kilometres long. Although it is the second longest river, the Amazon is the biggest because it holds the most water.

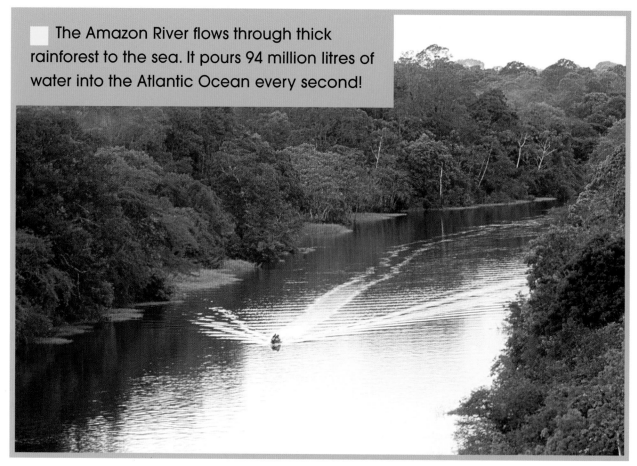

The Amazon River flows through thick rainforest to the sea. It pours 94 million litres of water into the Atlantic Ocean every second!

The water cycle

Rivers are part of the **water cycle**. When rain falls onto the land, some soaks into the ground or is taken in by plants. Rainwater also collects in lakes and ponds, and flows from streams and rivers into the sea. When this water **evaporates**, it rises into the air where it forms clouds and falls back to the ground as rain, sleet or snow.

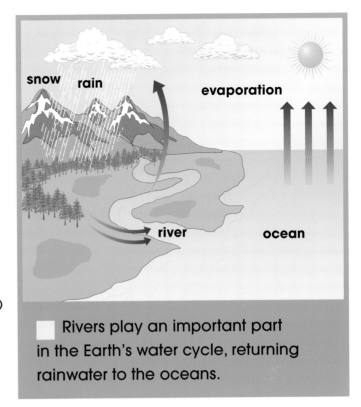

Rivers play an important part in the Earth's water cycle, returning rainwater to the oceans.

River water

The water that flows in rivers comes from rainwater, melted snow and natural streams called **springs**. Small streams run downhill and join together to form rivers. Smaller rivers and streams that run into a bigger river are called **tributaries**.

Mountain streams run quickly over rocks down a mountain. They join together to form a river.

All along a river

The force of **gravity** pulls things towards the centre of the Earth. This makes river water flow downhill towards the sea. The flowing water is full of **energy** and constantly changes the shape and size of the river.

A river's course

The route of a river is called its course. It begins in high ground at the **source**. The highest part of a river, the upper course, is narrow and fast flowing. In the middle course, the river becomes wider and deeper. In the lower course, the river flows more slowly, curving over flat ground.

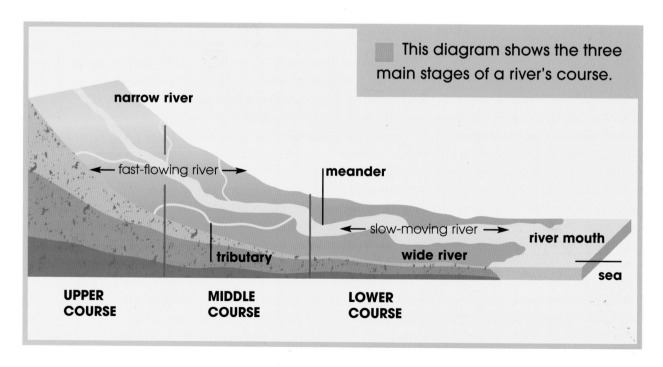

This diagram shows the three main stages of a river's course.

narrow river

← fast-flowing river →

meander

← slow-moving river →

river mouth

tributary

wide river

sea

UPPER COURSE

MIDDLE COURSE

LOWER COURSE

A river's mouth

The mouth of a river is where the water flows into the sea. This area is called an **estuary**. Some rivers drop **sediment** as they reach the sea. If the sediment splits the river into separate channels, a **delta** forms.

This river has dropped sediment as it approaches the sea, creating a triangular-shaped delta.

Make a model river course

You will need:
- large rectangular tray
- self-hardening clay
- modelling tools to carve the clay • waterproof paints • jug of water

1 At one end of the tray, build a clay mountain with steep slopes at the top, gentle slopes lower down and a flat base.

2 Carve a river course down your mountain. Make it narrow at the top and wider at the bottom.

Add clay rocks for the river to flow over.

3 Paint your river course with blue and green paints, with some white or silver specks for foam and sunlight on the water. Leave to dry.

4 Pour water slowly into the top of your river course. Watch the water follow the course down the mountain.

Wearing away the land

Over many years, rivers **erode** the ground they flow over. They can create deep channels called gorges or canyons, and dramatic waterfalls.

Gorges and canyons

Erosion takes place when river water carries along soil, sand and loose stones. These materials scrape and carve out the banks, or sides, of the river and the river bed or bottom. Over many years, this makes the river deeper and wider.

The Colorado River helped to form the Grand Canyon in the USA over a period of six million years.

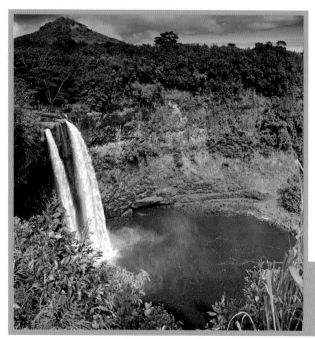

Waterfalls

Waterfalls form in the upper course of a river, where hard and soft rock meet. The water wears the soft rock away, leaving a ledge of hard rock. The river tumbles over the ledge to make a waterfall.

This waterfall has worn away a basin beneath it called a plunge pool.

Create a collage waterfall

Ask an adult to help you with this activity

You will need:
- shoe box • glue or sticky tape • scissors • waterproof paints • green tissue paper
- plastic (from a large sandwich bag)
- bubble wrap

1 Take the lid off the shoe box and put it over a narrow side of the box to make an L-shape. Glue or tape it in place. Ask an adult to cut the sides of the box to make it look like the edges of a river bank.

2 Paint the box brown and green to look like rocks and plants around a waterfall. Paint the bottom (inside) green and blue for the plunge pool.

3 Cut the green tissue paper to make feathery ferns and water plants and glue them to the inside edges of the box.

4 Cut the plastic into long ribbons and stick them to the top of the lid so they dangle down into the plunge pool and create a waterfall. You could add some bubble wrap to your pool to look like foam from the falling water.

Flood plains

Flood plains are found along the lower course of a river, where the water flows slowly and the land on either side is flat.

Rich farmland

When heavy rain falls, or water from melted snow flows down from the mountains, the river swells and overflows onto its flood plain. Sediment made up of sand, soil and bits of rock in the river water drops onto the ground, creating rich farmland.

Farmland by the Yangtze River in China is good for growing crops.

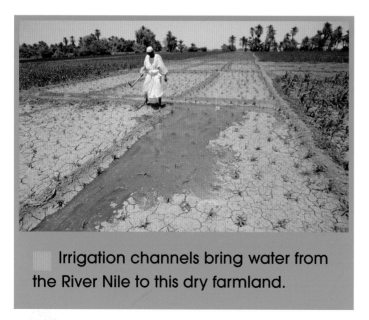

Irrigation channels bring water from the River Nile to this dry farmland.

Irrigation

The River Nile in Africa flows through areas of **desert** where it hardly ever rains. Farmers store the river water in **irrigation** channels. They use it to water their crops throughout the year.

Make a self-watering system

Ask an adult to help you with this activity

You will need:
- small plastic water bottle
- duct tape • felt-tip pen
- square of strong plastic about 10 cm x 10 cm (from a strong plastic bag) • pin
- elastic band • pot plant in soil • water

1 Remove the plastic lid from the bottle. Ask an adult to cut off the bottom of the bottle and to put duct tape over the sharp edge.

2 Draw around the bottle spout onto the square of plastic with the felt-tip pen. Ask an adult to make four or five small holes in the plastic circle with the pin.

3 Put the plastic over the bottle spout and secure it in place with an elastic band.

4 Turn the bottle upside down and push it into the soil next to the plant you need to water. Fill the bottle with water.

Your self-watering system stores water and helps to water your plant gradually. This is particularly useful if you have to go away for a few days. You could use larger bottles for outdoor plants.

Bends and loops

If you follow a river's course on a map, you will see that it does not travel in a straight line. As the river gets bigger, it bends and loops as the water weaves from side to side.

Meandering along

Meanders are bends in a river. The flow of water (the current) is faster around the outside of a bend and wears away the bank. On the inside of a bend, the slower current drops sediment and makes the bend bigger.

Oxbow lake

As the bends of a meander get bigger, they move towards each other. Sometimes the two bends meet and the river begins to flow between them. When this happens, the bend is cut off from the river and forms an oxbow lake.

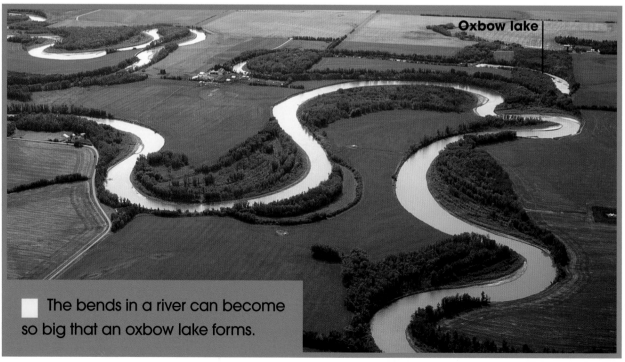

Oxbow lake

The bends in a river can become so big that an oxbow lake forms.

Play 'Pooh sticks'

Use this activity to find out which parts of a river have the strongest current.

Two adults must be present during this activity at all times

You will need:
• a friend • two adults
• stopwatch

1 Visit a small river or stream near to where you live, with a footbridge crossing over it.

2 Find two sticks. Push each stick through a large leaf to make them easy to recognise.

3 Mark a place about 20 metres downstream in the direction that the current is flowing. Make sure the bridge is still visible from this position. Ask your friend and an adult to stand by the mark with a stopwatch.

4 With an adult, take the sticks to the bridge. Shout 'Go!' as you drop one stick into the middle of the river and your friend starts the stopwatch.

5 How long does the stick take to reach the mark? Drop the other stick nearer the bank and do the same. Where is the current stronger? You could record your findings on a chart.

River plants

Many different kinds of plants grow in river beds, along river banks or in river water. Plants grow best in a slow-flowing river. A fast current may wash away soil and the plants that grow in it.

Along the banks

Willow trees often grow along river banks because they need to drink plenty of water. Their roots help to stop the banks eroding. When tall reeds grow close together by the river bank, they provide shelter for birds and river **mammals**.

Birds often build their nests amongst the reeds by a river bank.

Water lilies have flat leaves that float on the water to face the sunlight.

Plants in the water

Some water plants keep the river water healthy and full of **oxygen**. In fast-flowing water, plants growing up from the river bed have long, flexible stems. In slow-flowing water, some plants have flat leaves that float on the surface.

Paint a river plant picture

You will need:
- large sheet of paper
- several small sheets of paper • pencil • paints

1 With an adult, visit a local river (or research a river on the Internet) to learn about the plants that grow there. If you arrange a visit, you can sketch your river and the plants you see (or you could take photographs).

2 Paint a stretch of the river and the river banks on a large sheet of paper.

3 Paint the river plants on the small pieces of paper (or print your photographs). Use books or the Internet to find out the names of the plants.

4 Stick the plant pictures around the edge of your river painting and label them clearly. Draw arrows to show where the plants are found.

Weeping willow

Bull rushes

Marsh marigolds

Water lilies

Tape grass

17

River wildlife

Rivers provide food and shelter for all kinds of animals – fish, birds, **amphibians**, **reptiles**, mammals and insects. If there is a lot of wildlife using the river, it usually means that the water is clean and healthy.

Frogs and toads

Frogs and toads are amphibians that live in the water and on land. You might see them swimming in the water, hopping on the bank or sitting on a water lily leaf. They lay hundreds of eggs, called spawn, in the water that hatch into new frogs. Some spawn are eaten by fish and birds.

Frogs make their home in a river or pond. Their eggs hatch in the spring.

Mammals

Otters and beavers are river mammals. They dig their burrows in the banks of a river. Otters catch fish, frogs and birds to eat. Beavers eat the bark from trees. They use their sharp teeth to drag branches into the water to build a dam.

Beavers build a dam to collect flowing river water. The dam makes a large, safe pool for them to swim in.

Make a beaver's dam

You will need:
- deep rectangular tray
- stones and sticks
- self-hardening clay • jug of water • sheet of A3 paper
- waterproof paints

1 Build a wall with stones and sticks, about a third of the way along the tray.

2 Use the clay to fill any gaps. Leave a small gap in the middle of the dam for the water to trickle through.

3 Pour water slowly into the smaller space behind the dam and watch it collect and form a pool.

4 Paint a backdrop for your dam on the large sheet of paper, showing a forest with a family of beavers living there.

Using rivers

People have always lived by rivers. River water can be used for drinking and for washing. Farmers use it to water their crops. A healthy river is also full of fish to eat.

Water power

Flowing river water is full of energy that can be captured and used to make **electricity**. A concrete dam is built to store river water. Jets of water flow through spaces in the dam and turn **turbines** that help to make electricity.

Water is stored by a dam at this power station to help make electricity.

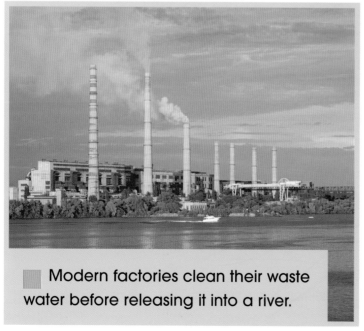

Modern factories clean their waste water before releasing it into a river.

Factories

Many factories are built on the banks of rivers. The river water is used to help make **goods**. But the waste water these factories produce can be full of chemicals. If it is poured back into the river, it will cause harm.

Make a water filter

Ask an adult to help you with this activity

You will need:
- large plastic bottle • scissors
- duct tape • paper kitchen towel • sand • gravel
- cotton-wool balls
- cooking oil • selection of foodstuffs (such as rice, oatmeal and tea leaves)
- jug of water • spoon

1 Ask an adult to help you cut the plastic bottle in half and put duct tape over the sharp edge. Take off the cap.

2 Put the top half of the bottle upside down into the bottom half to make a funnel. Add layers of filter materials to your funnel in the following order – a paper kitchen towel, a layer of sand, a layer of gravel, some cotton-wool balls.

3 Add a tablespoon of cooking oil and the foodstuffs to a jug of water and stir. Pour the mixture slowly through the filter.

The filter helps to separate out some of the foodstuffs. How clean is the water that comes through the filter?

River transport

Rivers are natural routes that can be used to transport people and goods. Wide, deep and very long rivers help ships and boats to travel inland. They load and unload at **ports** along the banks of the river.

Canals

Canals are man-made rivers. They were dug between towns and used to join up rivers before railways became a popular form of transport. Horses walked along **towpaths** to pull barges loaded with coal or other goods.

Barges used to be pulled along by a horse on the towpath.

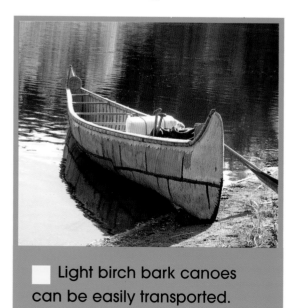
Light birch bark canoes can be easily transported.

River boats

Rivers have always been a popular place for people to settle, with transport so close to home. Many years ago, rafts, boats and canoes were only made from local materials. In Canada, for example, strong, light canoes were built from the soft bark of birch trees.

Make a birch bark canoe

You will need:
- A4 brown thin card or strong paper • pencil • scissors
- hole punch • string • thick card • glue or sticky tape
- felt-tip pens

1 Fold the card in half lengthways. Draw a line 2 cm above the centre fold. Fold back one side of the card along this line. Turn the card over and repeat.

2 Turn the card so the folds are along the bottom (in a kind of W-shape but with the middle fold much shorter). Flatten and draw on a canoe shape. Make sure the bottom edge of the card is the bottom of your canoe. Cut it out.

3 Punch four holes along each end. Thread the string through the holes and secure tightly.

4 Push down the centre fold to give your canoe a flat bottom. Cut two small strips of card and tape or glue them across the top of your canoe to make two seats.

5 Decorate your canoe with felt-tip pens. Cut out a paddle from the thick card, to match your canoe.

Enjoying rivers

There are lots of things to enjoy by a river, from rowing in a boat to walking along the river bank. There are fish to catch in the water and water birds to spot in the plants and trees.

River sports

Many people enjoy river sports to get fit and to have fun. Skilled sports include paddling canoes or rowing boats (with up to eight rowers) along straight, flat stretches of river.

In this competition, strong rowers are racing along a river.

A white water raft twists and turns along a raging river.

White water

Rivers tumble downhill over ridges and boulders, sending up spray and foam and creating 'white water'. People put on life jackets and go down the white water in rafts or canoes for a thrilling ride.

Play the great river race board game

You will need:
- large sheet of card
- pens and crayons • dice
- counters (or you could make little canoes, rafts and boats from self-hardening clay)

1 Copy the game shown below onto the card.

2 Take it in turns to roll the dice and move your counters across the board.

3 Follow the instructions on the squares you land on. The first to get to the sea is the winner! Can you make a river race board game of your own?

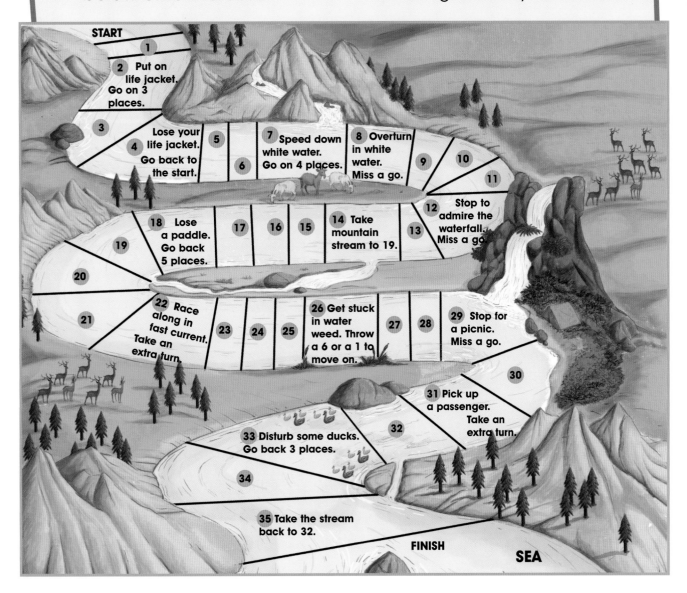

START
1
2 Put on life jacket. Go on 3 places.
3
4 Lose your life jacket. Go back to the start.
5
6
7 Speed down white water. Go on 4 places.
8 Overturn in white water. Miss a go.
9
10
11
12 Stop to admire the waterfall. Miss a go.
13
14 Take mountain stream to 19.
15
16
17
18 Lose a paddle. Go back 5 places.
19
20
21
22 Race along in fast current. Take an extra turn.
23
24
25
26 Get stuck in water weed. Throw a 6 or a 1 to move on.
27
28
29 Stop for a picnic. Miss a go.
30
31 Pick up a passenger. Take an extra turn.
32
33 Disturb some ducks. Go back 3 places.
34
35 Take the stream back to 32.
FINISH
SEA

Caring for rivers

Pollution and litter can harm rivers and the wildlife that depends on them. If some river plants grow too thick, they stop other wildlife growing. Everyone can get involved in keeping their local river clean and healthy.

Litter

Rivers and their banks are often used as dumping grounds for car tyres, shopping trolleys, traffic cones and other rubbish. Crisp packets and plastic bottles thrown away carelessly can clog up the water flow and harm river wildlife.

These fish have died because their river home has become polluted.

Harmful plants

Some river plants have been introduced from other countries. They can grow thick and tall, killing **native** plants and harming wildlife. Getting to know harmful plants and reporting them helps to control their growth.

Japanese knotweed grows on European river banks. It prevents the growth of native plants, erodes the banks and can cause flooding.

Adopt a local river

1 Get to know your local river and the plants and animals that live there.

2 Draw sketches or take photographs of the plants and animals that you see.

3 Find out about an organisation that cares for your local river (such as www.rivercare.org.uk). Join up yourself, or find out if your school will get involved. Help out with one of their projects to look after a river.

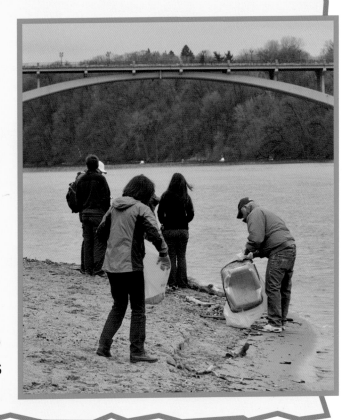

Glossary

amphibian

An amphibian is an animal that lives in water and on land.

channel

A channel is a trench or groove cut into the land. River water flows along channels.

delta

A delta is a flat, swampy area of land at a river's mouth. It is made when a river drops sediment as it approaches the sea.

desert

A desert is a rocky or sandy area of land with little rainfall.

electricity

Electricity is a kind of energy made in power stations. We use electricity in our homes to turn on lights and to work machines.

energy

Energy is the power to work. River water has lots of energy.

erode

Erode means to wear away.

estuary

An estuary is the mouth of a river, where river water mixes with sea water.

evaporates

Water evaporates when it turns into a gas called water vapour.

goods

Goods are items such as food or building materials that we transport from place to place.

gravity

Gravity is a force that pulls objects towards the Earth's centre.

irrigation

Irrigation is the supplying of water to crops growing in dry fields.

mammal

Mammals are animals with fur or hair. Mammal mothers feed their babies with their own milk.

native

Native plants or animals come from a particular place and have not come from elsewhere.

oxygen

Oxygen is a gas that almost all living things need to survive.

pollution

Pollution is when something is made dirty. River water can become polluted with litter or harmful chemicals.

port

A port is a place by the coast or a river bank where boats can load and unload people and goods.

reptile

A reptile has scaly skin and cold blood. Reptiles, such as snakes and crocodiles, need heat from the Sun to warm them up.

sediment

Sediment is the bits of earth and rock carried by river water.

source

The source of a river is the point where it begins.

spring

A spring is where water bubbles up from underground.

towpath

A towpath is a path beside the bank of a river or canal.

tributaries

Tributaries are rivers or streams that join a bigger river.

turbines

Turbines are wheels turned by flowing water or air to make energy.

water cycle

The water on Earth goes round and round in a water cycle. Water falls as rain and runs into rivers and the sea. The water evaporates to make clouds and falls again as rain.

Index

Amazon 6
animals 16, 18, 19, 24, 27

boat 22, 23, 24

canal 22
channel 6, 9, 10, 12, 28
Colorado 10
course 8, 9, 10, 12, 14
current 14, 15, 16

dam 19, 20
delta 9, 28

electricity 20, 28
energy 8, 20, 28
erosion 10
estuary 9, 28

flood plain 12, 14

gravity 8, 28

irrigation 12, 28

lake 7, 14

meander 8, 14

Nile 6, 12

oxbow lake 14

plants 7, 13, 16, 17, 24, 27
pollution 26, 29
port 22, 29

route 8, 22

sea 6, 7, 8, 9
sediment 9, 12, 14, 29
source 8, 29
spring 7, 29
stream 6, 7

transport 22
tributary 7, 8, 29
turbine 20, 29

water 6, 7, 8, 9, 10, 12, 14, 16,
    18, 19, 20, 24, 26
water cycle 7, 29
water filter 21
waterfall 10, 11

Yangtze 12